For Matt and Rach, with love - C.S.

For Mahni, as you spread your wings and soar xx - C.B.

*Wedge-tailed Eagle*
first published in 2024
by Walker Books Australia Pty Ltd
Gadigal and Wangal Country
Locked Bag 22, Newtown
NSW 2042 Australia
www.walkerbooks.com.au

Walker Books Australia acknowledges the Traditional Owners of the country on which we work, the Gadigal and Wangal peoples of the Eora Nation, and recognises their continuing connection to the land, waters and culture. We pay our respect to their Elders past and present.



NATIONAL LIBRARY OF AUSTRALIA

A catalogue record for this book is available from the National Library of Australia

ISBN: 978 1760655 68 6



The illustrations for this book were created digitally
Typeset in Fanwood and Pompiere
Printed and bound in China

10 9 8 7 6 5 4 3 2 1

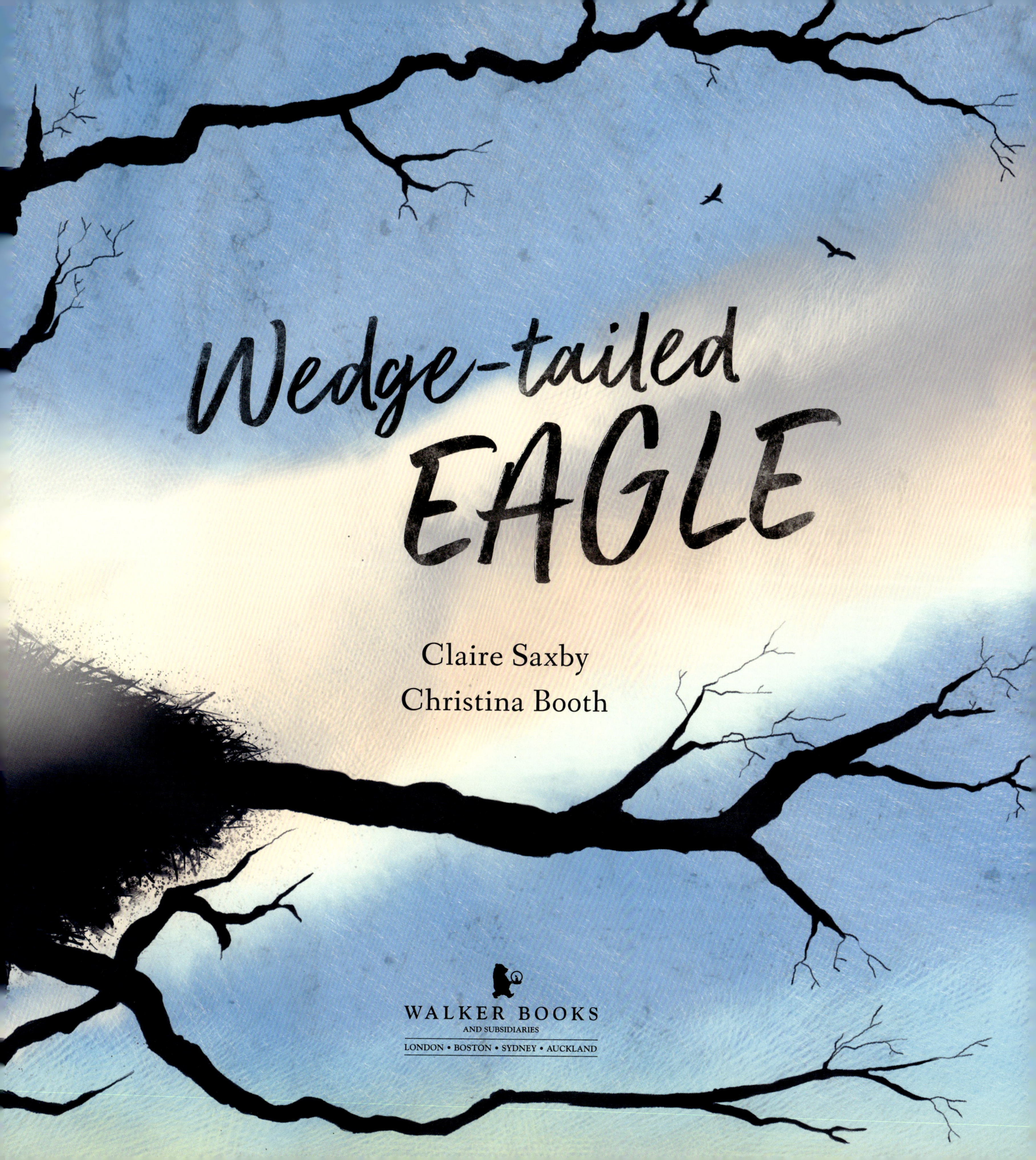

# Wedge-tailed EAGLE

Claire Saxby
Christina Booth

WALKER BOOKS
AND SUBSIDIARIES
LONDON • BOSTON • SYDNEY • AUCKLAND

Look up.

Way up, into the clear blue.
Those two tiny specks are a
wedge-tailed eagle and her mate.

Columns of rising air called 'thermals' form over plains where there is uneven heating. From heights of 2 kilometres or more, wedge-tailed eagles can see the boundaries of their territory. They can also see prey and carrion.

They hover, dark wings extended
and diamond tails flared.
Watch them fold wings and dive.

Down,
down,
down they plunge.

Only when it seems they must crash do they spread their wings and climb again.

Eagle spirals upwards on the thermal, her mate close by. On the next dive, they roll and parry, mock fighting with talons tucked into tight fists.

Wedge-tailed eagles perform a display called a 'pothook' to impress their mate at the beginning of a new breeding season. Thermals allow eagles to climb using very little energy. The flying and mock-battle ritual is also used to reinforce territory boundaries.

When they are done, Eagle and her mate settle side by side in a tree and groom each other.

This is a perfect spot to watch for prey. Here a wallaby. There a possum.

On the water, a duck.

Wedge-tailed eagles mate for life. This grooming is called allopreening and helps to keep their bond strong.

Wedge-tailed eagles are accurate and powerful hunters. They will also eat carrion – dead animals – such as roadkill.

Throughout their territory are several old nests. Eagle and her mate return to a nest they have used before. It is many years deep, strong and safe.

They gather branches and weave new into old, then top the nest with fresh leaves.

Nests are set high in trees with a long view, few low branches and some overhead shade. Wedge-tailed eagles may use the same nest for many years.

As nesting time approaches, Eagle hunts less.

Her mate prepares food and brings it to her.

Female wedge-tailed eagles are bigger than males and will gain more weight in preparation for egg-laying.

Eagle lays two brown-blotch eggs and settles in to keep them warm. For weeks, she and her mate share the daytime nesting.

Night-time nesting is hers alone.

From egg-laying to hatching takes about 45 days. Both female and male wedge-tailed eagles develop a bare strip on their belly called a brood patch, to keep eggs warm.

A goanna climbs their tree.

It is unlikely to reach the nest but they take no chances.

Eagle's mate attacks in a flurry of wings and extended talons until the goanna retreats.

Wedge-tailed eagles have few predators, but they must protect their eggs from other forest dwellers.

In the days before they hatch, Eagle can hear her chicks call from within their eggs. She soft-calls in response.

It's nearly time.

The chicks pip-pip-pip, each chipping away at the shell with their egg-tooth. Downy-white, black-eyed and long-toed, they are exhausted.

Egg-pipping is hard work.

The process of hatching from an egg is called 'pipping'. Adults do not assist in pipping.

Eagle protects the chicks while her mate hunts. He drops prey at the edge of the nest. She prepares fine strips for their fast-growing offspring.

The chicks squawk and snatch. They eat until they are full, then sleep until they are hungry.

They flap stubby wings and hop about the nest.

Wedge-tailed eagle chicks are about 100 grams at birth but will grow to about 500 grams in the first week. Between feeds, chicks sleep lying flat out in the nest. Parents may deliver food to the nest several times in a day.

Wedge-tailed eagles will leave the territory of their parents 6 to 9 months after hatching. For the next 4 to 5 years they may travel widely in the search for food and potential mates.

The chicks' first flight is to a nearby branch. Day by day they fly further and return less often. They follow their parents to carrion. They glide upwards on thermals.

And then they are gone.

Look up.

Way up, into the clear blue.
Those tiny specks are two
wedge-tailed eagles.

Watch them soar.

INFORMATION ABOUT

# Wedge-tailed Eagles

Wedge-tailed eagles are the largest raptor in Australia. They are found widely throughout Australia and southern Papua New Guinea. Male wedge-tailed eagles weigh up to four kilograms, with females heavier at up to five kilograms. They can be up to one metre tall and their wingspan can exceed two metres. Wedge-tailed eagles eat their prey whole then regurgitate as pellets the bits they can't digest. Young wedge-tailed eagles are gold-brown but as they mature, their feathers become darker.

## About the Author

Claire Saxby lives in Melbourne, Australia and loves her city. She is the bestselling and award-winning author of many books. *Big Red Kangaroo* and *Emu* (both illustrated by Graham Byrne) and *Koala* (illustrated by Julie Vivas) have won numerous awards including the Royal Zoological Society of NSW's Whitley Award, the Environment Award for Children's Literature and Children's Book Council of Australia (CBCA) Crichton Award. *Koala* was a CBCA Honour Book. *Dingo* (illustrated by Tannya Harricks) was joint winner of the Patricia Wrightson Prize for Children's Literature at the NSW Premier's Literary Awards (2019), won the Royal Zoological Society of NSW's Whitley Award (2018) and was shortlisted for Best Picture Book in the Educational Publishing Awards. Both of her most recent Nature Storybooks – *Great White Shark* (2022, illustrated by Cindy Lane) and *Tasmanian Devil* (2023, illustrated by Max Hamilton) – were winners of Whitley Awards.

## About the Illustrator

Author and illustrator Christina Booth works from her bush studio in Tasmania, Australia. Trained as a teacher and painter, she loves that she makes up stories and colours for a living. Christina started her literary career illustrating for great Australian authors such as Max Fatchen, Colin Thiele, Christobel Mattingley and Jackie French. Many of Christina's books have been CBCA Notables and her 2009 picture book *Kip* was a CBCA Honour Book. She won the 2014 Environment Award for Children's Literature for *Welcome Home,* and her 2019 title *One Careless Night* was shortlisted for the Prime Minister's Literary Awards, and won the Environment Award for Children's Literature and the Whitley Book Award.

# Index



Look up the pages to find out about all these wedge-tailed eagle things. Don't forget to look at both kinds of word – this kind and this kind.